This book is dedicated to all the brave Cyber Defenders
who work tirelessly and give up precious time with their
families and friends to keep the people online safe.

And to our young readers: We hope this book helps you
learn to appreciate the importance of cybersecurity
and that you might one day be inspired
to take up your sword and shield and join the fight.

Aviv Cohen

Chief Marketing Officer,
Pentera

Written by **Dana Meschiany**

Illustrated by **Idan Barzilay**

Special thanks to Adi Bar-Lev, Aviv Cohen and Ziv Almog
for their invaluable contributions to this book. Your creativity, expertise,
and dedication have made this project a success.
Thank you for sharing your knowledge and passion for cybersecurity
to help educate and empower young readers.

ISBN: 979-8-9880230-0-5

Graphic Design by **Nofar Kella**
Produced by **Publish Pros**

PENTERA PRESENTS

CASTLE DEFEND3RS

What Do Cyber Parents Do?

Emma and Oliver sat down for dinner,
as they do every night.
Daddy had made some yummy spaghetti,
but Mommy was nowhere in sight.

"Where's Mommy?" the kids asked.
"At work," Daddy replied.
"**OH, AGAIN**?" Oliver frowned.
"You both work so late," Emma sighed.

"Yes, that's true. You are right.
We do work very hard.
In our special world,
we are always on guard."

"What exactly do you DO?"
Emma wanted to know.
Daddy thought for a moment,
then put it just so:

"We all use phones and laptops
each and every day.
These devices make it easy
to chat, learn, and play."

"The pictures and messages
you share with your friends
travel through the internet
when someone clicks Send.

The internet is a connected web of fiber,
creating what we like to call

THE WORLD OF CYBER!"

"Some people in this world
want to take what you keep,
stealing your secrets
in one sneaky sweep.

These folks, we call them bad hackers,
are up to no good.
Someone needs to stop them
to protect our **cyber-hood**."

Daddy paused and
proudly raised his chin.
"Taking care of these bad hackers
is where we come in!

We are Cyber Defenders,
both Mommy and I,
protecting the cyber world
from every bad guy!"

"YOU'RE SUPERHEROES!"

Oliver cried, and Daddy gave him a grin.

"But we don't fly or wear capes.
Our power comes from within.
As Cyber Defenders, we ensure
the internet is safe for all."

"That sounds important," Emma said.
"Is that why you're always on call?"

"That's right! Every morning
Mommy and I go to work, side by side.
Bringing our laptops and cyber-tools
along for the ride.

Once we're there, we stop bad guys
from ever getting their way.
Using our smarts and our keyboards,
the fight goes on all day."

"So you're wizards," Oliver mused,
"With secret potions and charms!"

CADABRA

...ABRA

They jumped into Daddy's arms.

"Not even close!" Daddy laughed,
    as he twirled them around.
"In cybersecurity, my loves,
    there's no magic to be found!"

Daddy thought for a moment
and devised a clever tale
to explain how cyber defense works
and how the good guys prevail.

"Imagine you have a big castle
you defend with all your might,
as thieves try to break in
every day and every night."

"You are knights in armor,
brave and shining bright,
keeping the villains away
and doing what is right."

"Your castle is quite grand,
with many rooms to see,
colorful gardens and dark dungeons
full of mystery.

Just like in the cyber world,
it can be hard to know
who is your true friend
and who is your worst foe.

People may come to the castle
and say they're loyal knights, too,
but you have to be careful
because it isn't always true!"

"These thieves attack everyone,
their targets are big and small.
Fortune or age doesn't matter,
they want to take it all.

When a battle first begins,
anything can go wrong.
Your castle walls might get breached
if you haven't made them strong."

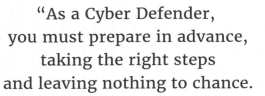

"As a Cyber Defender,
you must prepare in advance,
taking the right steps
and leaving nothing to chance.

Put on your helmets,
and keep your shields at hand,
be strong and get ready
to take a brave stand."

"Close the drawbridge!"

"Lock the gates!"

"Let no one shady get by!"

"Keep watch, sound the horns, find and capture every spy."

Emma and Oliver's
imagination ran wild
as Daddy paused
with a playful smile.

"Tell us more Daddy!"
they pleaded and cried.
Daddy smirked,
and then he replied:

"Sometimes these crooks
still find a way in,
seeking to cause
harm from within."

"They go unnoticed at first, in disguise,
so it's up to you to detect these bad guys.

You need to act fast,
and respond with all your might!
Stand up, even if it's scary,
in a spectacular fight!"

"To make your fortress secure once more,
mend all that's broken and lock every door.
Check every nook and repair all the fences,
rebuild your walls and strengthen defenses."

Emma and Oliver had many suggestions:

"Can we add loud alarms for extra protection?"

"Build a moat with crocodiles to scare them away?"

"Camouflage our castle
to lead bad guys astray?"

"Your ideas are awesome!
I love how you think.
These robbers are crafty.
They'll fool you in a blink!
You must be one step ahead
of the tricks they may use,
otherwise they will take
anything that they choose."

"But how?"

Emma asked, feeling unsure.
"How can we make it completely secure?"

"To keep your treasures safe and sound,
you must think like a thief and look around.
If you can get in, then they can too,
so look for the places they might get through.
Find the spots where they can sneak in and hide,
then patch them so they can't even peek inside."

Oliver piped up,
"That sounds cool and so clear!
We'll keep our fortress safe
without a shred of fear!"

At that exact moment,
Mommy came in from outside.
Emma and Oliver ran to her
and said with such pride:

"Daddy told us what being
a Cyber Defender is about!"
Mommy chuckled and asked,
"Well, what did you find out?"

"As Cyber Defenders, you have a big role,
keeping the cyber world safe and whole.

With your keyboard a sword,
your knowledge a shield,
you protect the people online,
refusing to yield!
That's why you are late
and always on call,
you're making the cyber world
safer for all!"

"When you grow up,
you can join us in our fight.
But for now, we can all guard
our castle tonight!"

They raised their hands high, cheering loud and long:
"We are CYBER DEFENDERS! Together we're strong!"

Already in bed,
under their covers for the night,
Emma turned to her dad
as he shut off the light.

"Daddy, there's just one thing
on which I don't agree.
Being a Cyber Defender
does seem magical to me!"

Daddy kissed her forehead and smiled,
while Mommy tucked them in tight.
"Cyber-safe dreams, our little ones.
Don't let the computer bugs bite!"

EMMA AND OLIVER'S 10 CYBER RULES TO STAY SAFE ONLINE

1. USE A SECRET PASSWORD KNOWN ONLY BY TRUSTED ADULTS, LIKE MOMMY AND DADDY.

2. PASSWORDS ARE PRIVATE, DON'T SHARE THEM WITH FRIENDS.

3. DON'T OPEN EMAILS FROM SOMEONE YOU DON'T KNOW OR WITH UNUSUAL SUBJECT LINES.

4. ASK BEFORE DOWNLOADING A NEW GAME OR APP.

5. DON'T CLICK LINKS IN EMAILS FROM FRIENDS OR FAMILY IF YOU AREN'T EXPECTING TO RECEIVE ONE.

6. DON'T TALK TO STRANGERS ONLINE, JUST LIKE YOU WOULDN'T TALK TO THEM IN REAL LIFE.

7. TREAT OTHERS WITH KINDNESS, BOTH ONLINE AND IN PERSON.

8. DON'T SHARE YOUR NAME, ADDRESS, OR PICTURES WITH STRANGERS ONLINE.

9. ONLY VISIT WEBSITES YOU KNOW ARE SAFE AND SECURE.

10. IF SOMETHING ONLINE MAKES YOU FEEL UNCOMFORTABLE OR UNSAFE, TELL A TRUSTED ADULT RIGHT AWAY. THEY'RE THERE TO PROTECT YOU!